A GRAPHIC HISTORY OF THE AMERICAN WEST

THE BATTLE OF THE LITTLE BIGHORN

BY GARY JEFFREY
ILLUSTRATED BY NICK SPENDER

Gareth Stevens
Publishing

Please visit our website, www.garethstevens.com.
For a free color catalog of all our high-quality books,
call toll free 1-800-542-2595 or fax 1-877-542-2596.

Library of Congress Cataloging-in-Publication Data

Jeffrey, Gary.
The Battle of the Little Bighorn / Gary Jeffrey.
p. cm. — (A graphic history of the American West)
Includes index.
ISBN 978-1-4339-6733-7 (pbk.)
ISBN 978-1-4339-6734-4 (6-pack)
ISBN 978-1-4339-6731-3 (library binding)
1. Little Bighorn, Battle of the, Mont., 1876—Juvenile literature. 2. Dakota
Indians—Wars—Juvenile literature. I. Title.
E83.876.J44 2012
973.8'2—dc23
2011022747

First Edition

Published in 2012 by
Gareth Stevens Publishing
111 East 14th Street, Suite 349
New York, NY 10003

Copyright © 2012 David West Books

Designed by David West Books

Photo credits:
p5t, National Archives

Printed in China

CPSIA compliance information: Batch #DW12GS: For further information contact Gareth Stevens, New York, New York at 1-800-542-2595.

CONTENTS

Native American peoples had lived on the continent for more than 12,000 years.

In the years after independence, the United States economy grew fast. Farmers wanted the territory to the south to grow cotton on and lobbied the government hard to get it.

FORCED OUT

When Andrew Jackson looked south, he saw fertile, empty lands that weren't being used. In 1830, he signed the Indian Removal Act. This allowed the government to arrange the removal to the west of all tribes east of the Mississippi. Their destination was a new "Indian Territory" (modern-day Oklahoma). Thousands of Native Americans died on a forced march called the "Trail of Tears."

President Andrew Jackson—architect of the Indian Removal Act

Alongside hostility, there was also keen interest in the culture and traditions of Native Americans. This illustration of a Mandan was made in 1834.

4

ALL ROADS WEST

The Homestead Act of 1862 allowed settlers to claim lands west of the Mississippi. The Great Plains were home to fierce tribes like the Cheyenne, Arapaho, and Sioux. Many white settlers believed in "manifest destiny"—a god-given right to settle the wilderness. When settlers and miners cut trails through Indian hunting grounds, wars broke out.

Lieutenant Colonel George Custer's expedition to the Black Hills of South Dakota in 1874 discovered gold. Even though the area was officially off limits, a gold rush began.

THE BATTLE FOR PAHA SAPA

Paha Sapa—the Black Hills of South Dakota—were sacred to the Lakota Sioux people and were protected by a treaty. The Lakota were hunters who followed the buffalo but used the Black Hills for game in the winter. The government needed to open the hills to mining. They ordered all free-roaming tribes to move onto a reservation. The Lakota and Cheyenne on the plains refused. In the spring of 1876, a huge force of cavalrymen, 600 of them led by Custer, was sent to bring them in...

Sitting Bull of the Lakota Hunkpapa was leader of the renegade Lakota and Cheyenne.

Custer was called "Long Hair" by the Plains tribes.

THE BATTLE OF THE LITTLE BIGHORN

SUNDAY, JUNE 25, 1876, 3:30 P.M. EAST OF THE LITTLE BIGHORN RIVER, MONTANA TERRITORY.

I DON'T BELIEVE IT! WE'VE GOT THEM – IT'S SITTING BULL'S VILLAGE!

IT WAS MORE THAN CUSTER COULD HAVE HOPED FOR.

NORMALLY HIS MEN WOULD HAVE BEEN **SPOTTED** AND HELD **BACK** BY AN ADVANCE GUARD OF WARRIORS WHILE THE VILLAGE SCATTERED. BUT NOT **TODAY**.

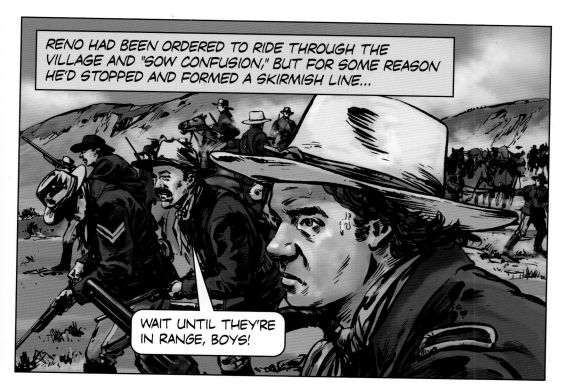

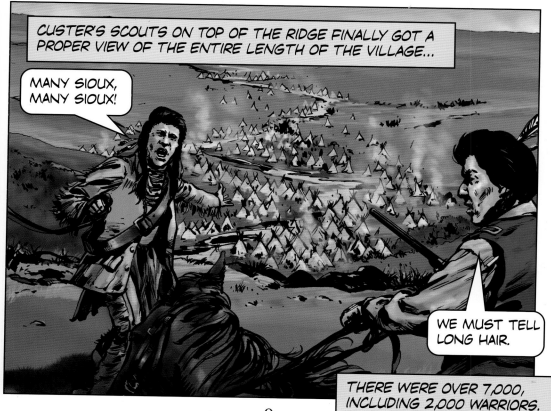

AFTER HEARING THE SCOUTS, CUSTER ORDERED A MESSAGE SENT...

ALRIGHT, I GOT IT...

CUSTER HAD EARLIER SENT COLONEL BENTEEN AND HIS BATTALION AWAY TO THE SOUTH TO GET A BETTER VIEW OF THE VILLAGE.

..."BENTEEN, COME ON, BIG VILLAGE, BE QUICK, BRING AMMUNITION..."

RIDE AS FAST AS YOU CAN. TAKE THE SAME ROUTE WE JUST TOOK!

IN THE OGLALA CIRCLE, CRAZY HORSE CAREFULLY PUT ON HIS WAR PAINT AS HIS WARRIORS WAITED.

AS LAKOTA WAR CHIEF, IT WAS CRAZY HORSE'S JOB TO LEAD THE WARRIORS INTO BATTLE.

CRAZY HORSE ASSEMBLED HIS WARRIORS ABOVE RENO'S POSITION...

CALM YOUR PASSION, WE NEED TO FIGHT AS ONE!

...AND CHARGED.

WHEEEEEEEEEEEEEEE!

HOKAHE!

AS THEY CHARGED, THE WARRIORS SOUNDED THEIR SHRILL EAGLE BONE WHISTLES.

CUSTER HALTED HIS MEN. EVEN THOUGH RENO'S CHARGE HAD **FAILED**, THERE WAS **HOPE**.

THE WARRIORS' FAMILIES ARE GATHERED ACROSS THE RIVER. IF WE CAN **CAPTURE** THEM, WE CAN STILL WIN THIS!

CUSTER DIVIDED HIS FORCE AGAIN, LEAVING MEN BEHIND UNDER CAPTAIN KEOGH TO HOOK UP WITH BENTEEN.

IN THE VILLAGE, THE WARRIORS WHO HAD DEFEATED RENO WERE ADDRESSED BY SITTING BULL...

A BIRD ON THE NEST **SPREADS** ITS WINGS TO **COVER** ITS EGGS AND **PROTECT** THEM!

14

CHEYENNE WARRIORS LEAPT FROM THE SAGEBRUSH TO SHOOT DOWN THE LEAD MAN.

BANG!

WHGHEHEHEHE!

THE TROOPS WHEELED THEIR HORSES AROUND AND RODE BACK UP TOWARD CUSTER.

CUSTER WAS BECOMING IMPATIENT...

WHERE ON EARTH IS BENTEEN? WE NEED **REINFORCEMENTS** TO TAKE THIS VILLAGE!

BUT BENTEEN WAS BUSY HELPING SAVE RENO'S COMMAND. HE WASN'T COMING.

A THIN LINE CONNECTED CUSTER'S AND KEOGH'S TROOPS. CRAZY HORSE DASHED BRAVELY IN BETWEEN, SPLITTING THE LINE IN TWO...

HOKAHE! YIP! YIP!

AAAAGH!

BANG!

BANG!

THE SOLDIERS SHOT HORSES TO MAKE BARRICADES FOR A BRAVE **LAST STAND**.

CUSTER STOOD WITH HIS BROTHERS, BOSTON AND TOM, AS THE SIOUX AND CHEYENNE **CLOSED IN**.

THEN CUSTER GOT SHOT IN THE CHEST. BEFORE HE DIED, HE LOOKED AROUND AT THE FEW REMAINING MEN WHO WERE STILL ALIVE.

BUT SOON...

ALL THE WHITE MEN ARE DEAD!

THE END

After destroying Custer, the Native Americans set about besieging Reno and Benteen. They both survived and were the first to reach the battlefield of the last stand. News of Custer's defeat came out the day after the centennial and sent a shock wave through white America.

ROUNDED UP

The battle was a disaster for the renegade Sioux and Cheyenne, too. They found themselves hunted as outlaws by the full might of the US Army. After spending time exiled in Canada, Sitting Bull finally led his bands onto the reservation in 1881. The Comanche of East Texas, the Apache of Arizona—by 1890 all free-roaming tribes had been confined to reservations. The West had finally been won for the settlers.

Chief Sitting Bull poses with Buffalo Bill Cody in 1885. Almost as soon as it ended, the time of the Old West became a myth.

One of the last to hold out was Geronimo. A famous leader of the Apache, Geronimo surrendered in 1886.

No longer allowed to hunt, Native Americans lived on handouts and under strict rules on reservations.

GLOSSARY

battalion A large military unit consisting of two or more companies or batteries.

bluffs Steep cliffs, riverbanks, or headland.

coulee A deep ravine with sloping sides, often dry in summer.

culture The behavior patterns, beliefs, and way of life of a particular community or era.

fertile Rich in material needed for plant growth.

lobbied Tried to persuade a government or a group of people to agree with a particular point of view.

myth A story or popular belief, associated with a particular person or hero, that often illustrates a cultural idea.

pandemonium Wild uproar, confusion, or chaos.

renegade A rebel, deserter, or outlaw.

reservation An area of land "reserved" for and governed by Native Americans.

shrill A very high pitched, piercing sound.

skirmish line A group of soldiers sent ahead of the main troops, positioned in a line to disrupt the enemy before battle.

INDEX